PERSIAN CATS

by Mari Schuh

AMICUS HIGH INTEREST • AMICUS INK

Amicus High Interest and Amicus Ink are imprints of Amicus
P.O. Box 1329, Mankato, MN 56002
www.amicuspublishing.us

Library of Congress Cataloging-in-Publication Data
Schuh, Mari C., 1975- author.
Persian cats / by Mari Schuh.
    pages cm. -- (Favorite cat breeds)
Audience: K to grade 3.
Summary: "A photo-illustrated book for early readers about Persian cats. Describes the Persian's unique features, history as good house pets, their social behaviors, and how they are the most popular and oldest breeds of cat"-- Provided by publisher.
Includes bibliographical references and index.
ISBN 978-1-60753-970-4 (library binding)
ISBN 978-1-68152-099-5 (pbk.)
ISBN 978-1-68151-004-0 (ebook)
1. Persian cat--Juvenile literature. 2. Cat breeds--Juvenile literature. I. Title.
SF449.P4S38 2017
636.8'32--dc23
                    2015028770

Photo Credits: GlobalP/iStock cover; Life On White/Exactostock-1598/ Superstock 2; Valerio Pardi/123rf 5; Lanmas/Alamy Stock Photo 6-7; Bestzmile/iStock 8-9; Tierfotoagentur/Alamy Stock Photo 10; kevinjeon00/iStock 12-13; blickwinkel/Alamy Stock Photo 14; Zanna Holstova/Shutterstock 17; fotojagodka/iStock 18-19; pyotr021/iStock 21; Eric Isselee/Shutterstock 22-23

Editor: Wendy Dieker
Designer: Tracy Myers
Photo Researcher: Rebecca Bernin

Printed in the United States of America.

HC 10 9 8 7 6 5 4 3 2 1
PB 10 9 8 7 6 5 4 3 2 1

For Liz and Rich—MS

TABLE OF CONTENTS

QUIET CATS

A fluffy cat lies on a sofa. Its owner combs the cat's fur. The cat is quiet. It is gentle. The cat is a Persian.

HISTORY

Persians likely came from Persia. Persia is now called Iran. Persian cats from long ago looked different. They had longer faces.

Fun Fact

Almost everybody knows and loves Persian cats. They are one of the most popular breeds.

SWEET FACES

Persian cats today have **unique** faces. Their faces are flat. They have big, round eyes. Their noses are short.

BEAUTIFUL FUR

A Persian has long, silky fur. It can be different colors and patterns. A Persian has a short, fluffy tail. Long fur covers its neck. It is called a **ruff**.

GROOMING

A Persian needs to be combed every day. This gets rid of loose hair. It keeps hair from getting **matted**. These cats should have a bath at least once a month.

KITTENS

Persian kittens change as they grow. Their eye color may change. Fur on black kittens gets darker. Markings on some kittens fade away.

Like a Wild Cat?

Lion cubs are born with spots. Like the fur on Persian kittens changes, spots go away as the cubs grow up.

PLAYING AND RELAXING

A Persian can be playful. It can be curious. But it rarely jumps or climbs. It often relaxes for a long time.

Fun Fact
Persians can be quiet and still. These cats are called "furniture with fur."

RESTFUL AND CALM

Persians are restful. They seem to enjoy calm homes. Persians do not get lonely when they are alone. But they can **adapt** to busy homes, too.

Like a Wild Cat?

Wild cats rest most of the day. Housecats do, too.

LOVING PETS

Persian cats enjoy getting

attention. But they do not beg

for it. They will sit on their owner's

laps. Owners cuddle with their

loving pets.

HOW DO YOU KNOW IT'S A PERSIAN?

big, round head

big, round eyes

long, flowing fur

flat face, short nose

short, thick legs

WORDS TO KNOW

adapt – to change for a different situation

attention – playing and being with someone or something

breed – a type of cat

matted – when fur turns into a thick, tangled lump

ruff – a ring of long hair around a cat's neck

unique – one of a kind or special

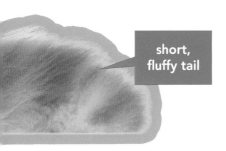

short, fluffy tail

LEARN MORE

Books

Dash, Meredith. *Persian Cats.* Cats. Minneapolis: Abdo Kids, 2015.

Felix, Rebecca. *Persians.* Cool Cats. Minneapolis: Bellwether Media, 2016.

Websites

Cat Fanciers' Association: For Kids
kids.cfa.org/index.html

Discovery Kids: Top Cats
discoverykids.com/articles/top-cats/

INDEX